Dear Simone,

WAIST DOES NOT EQUAL WORTH

The Curvy Doc's Guide to Positive Self Esteem

JANELLE SIMMONS

God placed you in my life when I needed a great sister and friend, someone who would always pray for me. You are a smart and amazing woman! Keep doing great things! I love you, more than you'll ever know. The Curvy Doc

Waist Does Not Equal Worth-The Curvy Doc's Guide to Positive Self Esteem

DEDICATION

This book is dedicated to my entire family. Mom: Thank you for believing in me and being my biggest cheerleader.

Dad-Heaven gained a great man. I hope I'm still making you proud.

ACKNOWLEDGMENTS

Thank you, God, for whom all blessings flow. Thank you for giving me the strength as I wanted to give up so many times.

To my family and friends-Thank you for putting up with me through the good, the bad, and the ugly. Your continued love and support means the world!

Moni Brodie-you are such an inspiration! Thank you for the opportunity to represent your brand and for agreeing to write the foreword; love you!

Sharlrita Deloatch-Thank you for encouraging me and helping me get this book out! You saw me laugh, you saw me cry...I'm grateful and so glad you were put in my path.

To my Sorors of Zeta Phi Beta Sorority, Inc.-Thank you for being my biggest group of supporters! Soror Yolanda Jarrett-had you never sent me the flyer for the model call, I would not be here now.

To my pageant families-Thank you for taking a chance on me.

To Tawana Blassingame and Philip Drew- Thank you for believing in me. You both laid the foundation for my blog, which hassince metamorphosized into this book.

Keith Burroughs, Sr.-You got my brand going and I will be forever grateful. Thank you for the constant words of encouragement

Keah Cher'i- You already know...love ya to pieces!

Amber Johnson and Azia Harris-Thank you for seeing my true potential before I even saw it in myself.

To the photographers, make-up artists, and stylists I have worked with-Thank you for making me look good each and every single time.

To my fans: THANK YOU! This is just the beginning so stay tuned!

TABLE OF CONTENTS

FOREWORD

As women we are often told it's important to love ourselves so that we don't allow others to mistreat us or devalue our worth; there is nothing but truth in that sentiment. However, what happens when the person that tells you the opposite is the one staring at you in the mirror. No matter what anyone ever says, it is your voice that will play the loudest in your head. Whether or not you can accomplish your dreams is all based on what you think about yourself. I can remember a time when I blamed everyone except me for any failure in my life…that man, that friend, that boss, the complete stranger when in reality it was ME. I'm so proud to say that over the years I've learned to be my biggest cheerleader instead of my biggest critic and once I made that switch, the sky was the limit. It was through my own transition that I began to notice in others the residue of a negative self-image. It took so much for me to become the woman I am today and although it can be a fight to block the voices in my own head telling me I am not enough, I do it and always come out on the other side.

I can remember like yesterday the first time I met Janelle. I was searching for fresh faces to represent my cosmetics line, Moni B.

Cosmetics and held a model call at a local Durham photography studio. Having been in North Carolina for over 10+ years I should've known better than to move forward with the call after hearing the forecast of snow but, I didn't want to reschedule. To my surprise there were several ladies that showed up that day and Janelle was one of them. On the outside she was amazing, dope, and fly, but on the inside she was struggling to keep it together. I could tell because she was me at one point in my life. Don't get me wrong she didn't walk into the room with her head held down as a matter of fact she walked in with a smile on her face but when you know….well, you just know. I knew that I wanted to be sure to include plus size beauties in my brand so, I was specifically looking for just a couple that day. Prior to Janelle's entrance into the room I had already selected 2 plus size models and although I had already met my goal but there was something about her that said 'you need her'.

Since that day in 2015, Janelle has blossomed in a way that makes me speechless every time I see her accomplish something new. From participating and winning a title in the NC Ms. Full Figured Pageant to serving as a sought after model and brand ambassador for others she has made her mark on the industry. Through loss, disappointment, and even adversity Janelle has been able to hold on to her purpose and soar. Circumstances that could have meant sure defeat for someone else, she's used as motivation to keep climbing. I'm so proud to take this journey right along with her as she continues to follow her dreams and live an amazing life that shows others the power in believing in your own greatness.

Moni B

THE BEGINNING

I was always a big girl. Growing up, I had to shop in the chubby girl section at Woolworth's. I was made fun of at school and was always the last person to be chosen in my physical education classes. Being a big girl wasn't an issue for me at such a young age. So what I was bigger than the other kids? It wasn't until the name calling got worse and my elders would start talking about my weight that I became self-conscious. I started hating what I saw in the mirror.

I hated I couldn't wear the fashionable clothes (or so I thought). I hated that my belly was so big, and my hips were too wide. My thighs…HATED THEM! My stretch marks… YUCK! I even hated my feet because they were big too. The only thing I loved about myself was my smile. I have full lips and a dimple on my left cheek (I got it from my Daddy). I always wore black clothing because it's a slimming color. I wore skirts on special occasions only. I didn't wear clothing that accentuated my curves.

I was a chubby toddler.

Let's not talk about the summer months. I wore shorts but they were below the knee and baggy. I wore a one-piece with a cover up on the beach. As I got older and started traveling internationally, I dreaded being around people in a swimsuit. I was ashamed. Black women are usually afraid about getting their hair wet in the pool; my fear was the men wanting to play water wars and them not being able to pick me up and throw me in the water.

I was a late bloomer when it came to dating and relationships, which could have been due to my low self-esteem. I attributed being single to my weight. I was constantly told, "you're beautiful BUT you could lose a few pounds." When I moved to the South from NYC in 2006, I was sure I was going to get snatched up by a Southern gentleman and get married because I heard men love big girls in the South. Well…I'm still single. Up until a couple of years ago, I thought I was the biggest, ugliest person on earth. Who would want to be with me? I used to always watch what I ate on a date. If I invited a man to my house and I cooked, I would put a very small portion on my plate. I dare not get seconds. I started to seek validation from men, giving more than I received. I wanted them to like me and to stay with me. I was told by a guy once that he wasn't used to dating women "like me". He was used to women that had Selma Hayek's shape. Hearing that immediately made me feel inadequate.

When it came to sex, the lights were off. Unfortunately, I was screwed (no pun intended) if I had sex in the daytime because I couldn't hide in darkness. Then there was that one night I decided to be daring and wear sexy lingerie. One word: HORRIBLE. I wanted to surprise my significant other at the time by greeting him at the door in a sexy lace teddy. It was crotch less and there were no cups for my breasts, so I was "roaming freely", breasts fully exposed. I wore black heels, and was excited to see the look on his face when I opened the door. The doorbell rang, and I was hyped and ready. I walk to the door, trying to keep calm. I opened the door expecting my significant other to grab me and start kissing every nook and cranny of my body; kind of what you see in the movies. Instead, I was met with laughter.

I had to quickly compose myself as I was thrown off guard. I asked the reason for the laughter and he said he wasn't laughing at me but WITH me. Huh? It was at that moment I vowed to never try and be sexy in the bedroom. That incident ended my relationship with lingerie. I was rejected and it made me hate my body even more. Many of you are probably reading this saying "it wasn't you; it was him". You're right; however I take partial responsibility because I allowed my low self-esteem to take control of the situation. I should have told him off and kicked him out when he started laughing, but instead I fed him dinner and had sex with him that night.

I vowed to never write again after completing my dissertation, so why this book? For one, results from a study done by Dove (the soap company) in 2016 showed that over half of the girls in the world do not have high body esteem and as a result avoid seeing friends and family, or attending outings. In addition, seven out of ten girls stop themselves from eating or otherwise put their health at risk. Two, and the main reason, is because of the messages I received once I started blogging my experiences as a curvy girl. Women related to my experiences. There are millions of people that struggle with low self-esteem, especially when it comes to body image. I wanted to share what has worked for me. I've fallen off the wagon a few times on my journey to self-love but I'm human. No one said the road would be easy.

I hope the following chapters help you become the best person you can be, regardless of size. There's a spot in the back to take notes. Sit back, relax, buckle your seat belt, and enjoy the ride!

I was chubby in high school too…LOL

THINGS HAPPEN
FOR A REASON

"Everything happens for a reason. Sometimes good things fall apart so better things can come together."

Marilyn Monroe

I truly believe things happen for a reason. For those who are religious, you were taught never to question God, and to trust His timing. Patience is a powerful virtue, one I have yet to master.

My experiences during my undergraduate years in college led me to a career in higher education administration, developing and implementing programs for students. I loved the students and the students loved me. I received numerous awards from professional organizations on my work; my dissertation focused on higher education. I loved what I did, and was ready to take my career to the next level. March 2015 I received the shock of my life when my contract was terminated unexpectedly at my job. I was extremely disappointed but figured I would bounce back quickly due to my skills and qualifications. Unfortunately, that did not happen. During this period not only was I fat and ugly, but broke too. I would not be employed again until ten months later.

As I was settling into my new job excited, but unsure of what the heck I was doing (my new job was not in higher education), one of my sorority sisters sent me a flyer about a model call for a local Black-owned cosmetics company. Many told me that I should pursue modeling; I thought they were crazy. Where did I fit into the modeling world? However, I figured I had nothing to lose so I went to the model call. It snowed that day and I kept saying to myself, "I should have stayed home", but I owed it to myself and my sorority sister to go through with it.

I interviewed with the CEO of Moni B Cosmetics, Moni Brodie (the lovely woman who wrote the foreword to this book), the model coordinator, and a photographer, who was responsible for taking photos of all of the model hopefuls. The interview wasn't too long; I took my photo and was informed I would be notified later that evening. I figured I wouldn't be selected so I didn't think much about it. As promised, Moni called me later that evening with news that surprised the hell out of me. Not only was I selected to be one of her models, but a brand ambassador as well! At the time, I didn't know what a brand ambassador was, but I was ecstatic! I had to wait until Moni made the official announcement before I shared on social media. I was sitting on my hands, eagerly waiting for the green light to post. Once the official announcement was made, I quickly followed my announcement on Facebook. In less than 24 hours, I received 490 likes (this was before the addition of the other reactions) and 92 comments. I couldn't believe it; folks were genuinely happy for me.

Janelle is wearing COCO LATTE and GOLD DIGGA

My first photo shoot with Moni B Cosmetics. Then…
(photo by Damien Prout)

And now…(photo by Moni Brodie)

The first time I saw my face in an ad at the mall. Yay!

walking in District of Curves fashion show
(photo by Pierre-Johnsons Photography)

Remembered how I started this chapter by saying things happen for a reason? If it wasn't for me losing my job, I would not have considered attending the model call. My previous work schedule would not have allowed me the opportunity. Modeling opened up opportunities I could have only imagined. Walking in fashion shows, being published in magazines (I even won a Plus Size Model of the Year Award) and an area I still cannot believe I explored, and love to this day-pageantry. I was named after pageant queen Janelle "Penny" Commissiong, the first Black Miss Universe who was crowned the year I was born. What also makes my name special is that she was from Trinidad and Tobago, the country of my heritage. I guess it was appropriate to explore this venture. It seems that many things I've done up to this point has been due to suggestions from others, In true Janelle fashion I didn't disappoint and gave it a chance. I didn't know there were beauty pageants for women that looked like me, so when I found out there was a fairly new plus size pageant in my area, I was eager to learn more information. I went to the audition not knowing what to expect and lo and behold, I was selected to compete.

I was so surprised at the number of people that were excited for me. I am thankful to my team that helped me get ready as I was clueless! I had so many people donate once, twice, THREE times to help me get everything I needed. Of course, I had some hiccups along the way but overall, I was very pleased leading up to the pageant. I could actually win this. However sadly I didn't. Well...let me rephrase that...I didn't win the overall title, but I placed first runner-up, and won numerous awards and titles so I served on the royal court. I received a crown and sash for my award, which was voted on by the audience and not the judges. That to me spoke volumes. This boosted my confidence, so much that I decided to compete in another pageant six months later. I didn't do well at all. I didn't place nor I win any awards...absolutely NOTHING. My flight to the pageant was canceled due to weather, so had to make the 10+ hour drive that same evening as I would have never made it to compete. Other factors played more of a minimal role, but I knew it wasn't my best. Instead of crying and feeling defeated, I was happy to have the experience behind me. The only thing I wished was that my dad (who had never seen me compete or even model at the time) was able to see me win something before he passed away. I truly understand that you can't win everything, but to not even get one award in front of him stung. I did bad, but not that bad.

After my first pageant. Didn't win the overall
prize but was a winner nonetheless.

Swimwear portion of pageant
(photography by Rick Jones)

I made a decision before the second pageant that I would stop competing. I had two different experiences and learned so much from them. Regardless of the outcomes, I have no regrets and love everyone that was a part of my journey. I love the pageant directors, staff, and fellow contestants. I also knew that I did not need a crown to become a queen. Besides, sometimes you hear more about the runners up than the actual winners themselves. In addition, pageantry is an expensive endeavor and after two pageants, finding sponsors became more of a challenge. And honestly, it wasn't something I considered doing for an extended period of time. I was encouraged by others; I did it and now it's over. Or so I thought…

A few months after the second pageant, I saw information about another pageant. I asked questions of people I knew who were reigning queens and I asked questions of the pageant director. I considered it, but did not decide to compete until a year later. It was while preparing for the third pageant that I unexpectedly lost my father. I was hoping he would have been able to attend, or at least be able to show him photos and hopefully have good news for him. Competing took a different meaning for me and for a few days, I was able to gather the strength to win the pageant in his honor. Third time really is a charm! Since winning I have become more interesting in learning about the inner workings of pageantry, to the point that my new business will consists of coaching pageant hopefuls. I've been asked if I will compete again. By the time you've read this book, I may have an answer.

Third times a charm! (Photography by W.T.M. Media)

You're probably wondering why in the world I just shared all of this, right? Because as devastating as losing my job...my career...was, the situation forced me to try new things which in turn, boosted my self-esteem. Sometimes you have to be placed in a situation in which you are forced to feel differently, and then over time, you start to believe those feelings. Modeling and pageantry forced me to stop feeling sorry for myself. I would be lying if I said I didn't occasionally have negative thoughts about myself; I'm human. However, those thoughts no longer control my life.

I challenge you to step outside of your comfort zone and be proud of it as that is a huge accomplishment in itself. Eventually, you will be proud of so much more.

THE POWER OF
THE TONGUE

*"Remember your words can plant gardens or
burn whole forests down."*

Gemma Troy

Words carry so much weight. How do you feel when you're insulted? Now imagine hearing something positive. Feels good, doesn't it?

The second step to positive self-esteem is changing your words, which in turn will change your mindset. What am I talking about? I am so glad you ask. I am talking about Self-affirmation. Self-affirmations are positive statements that assist in the challenging and eventual removal of negative thoughts. When you repeat them often, you start to believe in them, resulting in positive change. Common questions with self-affirmations include:

- What do I say?
- How do I say them?

- When do I say them?
- How many do I say?

There is no formal method to self-affirmations; you can do them however you like. But if you're struggling, try these:

1. Make a list of positive statements that you make to make true and place them in a visible location. Don't know what to say? Do a Google search or check Pinterest for examples.
2. Read the positive statements every day.
3. Look in the mirror when saying your self-affirmations.
4. Listen to self-affirming music; learn the words and sing them every day. Here are three I listen to regularly:
   a. Beautiful-Christina Aguilera
   b. Me Too-Megan Trainor
   c. Hot Girls-Lil' Mo featuring Lil' Wayne

When I started modeling and pageantry, I had to get myself together. A major part of participating in those activities required confidence. A picture says a thousand words, and those words are powerful.

I started looking in the mirror every morning, in addition to any moment in which I was placed in a position that required confidence. In modeling and pageantry, I use self-affirmations to get in the zone. I'm sure my pageant sisters thought I was being anti-social at times, but I needed that time to prepare my outside for what I was saying to my inside.

For those with children, it's very important to teach them self-affirmations. Bullying is at an all-time high in schools due to social media. Children as young as nine are ending their lives as a result of bullying. Lead by example and say self-affirmations with them. Confirm them with your children daily.

Don't beat yourself up if you have a bad day and regress to prior habits. Learning to love one-self is a process, so you will have bad days. As R&B songstress Aaliyah (RIP) sings "if at first you don't succeed, dust yourself off and try again." Don't give up, bounce back, and keep pushing!

LET THAT SHIT GO!

"Learn to let go. That is the key to happiness."

Buddha

Growing up I dreaded family gatherings because there was bound to be at least one person who would look at me and say, "You sure got bigger from when I last saw you", "Look at your (insert body part here)". That, along with other things that were said by different people over the years, had a negative effect on my self-esteem. I also hated hearing, "You know that's how so and so is", "They're just concerned", "Don't take it personal", etc. The intentions may have been good, but the damage has been done. Remember when I said in the last chapter regarding the more you say something the more you believe it? This applied to what was being said to me as well.

I prayed not to receive clothing as gifts because I would be embarrassed if they didn't fit. I didn't like shopping with others for that very reason. That's where my disgust for shopping stems from. Even though I'm in a much better space, I still never got into shopping. It's a stressful experience and my sense of style is nil. If I need an outfit for an event or trip, I wait until the very last minute to go to the department store. Sometimes, I shop online because it's done in the privacy of my own home. Going through racks of clothing gives me a headache.

After some of the things I've been told by men I dated or "talked to", who I thought cared about me, I equated not being good enough not just in love but at life. When I saw my friends winning, I was ecstatic for them, but it made me hate myself even more because had I been good enough, good things would happen to me too. I decided to give up at life and even contemplated suicide. Losing my job, a job in which I was recognized on a national level, and won awards for my work, now unemployed and useless.

You're probably wondering why I keep mentioning losing my job in this book on body positivity. I mentioned it to make a point. In order to move forward, I had to let the past go. In order for me to move forward professionally, I had to let go of the fact that I lost my job. I wasn't going to get the job back so why keep crying about it? How was I ever to achieve success if I continued to dwell in the past? How was I going to love myself if I let the words that other people said persist in destroying me? YOU'VE GOT TO LET THAT SHIT GO! As soon as I let go of that hurt and negativity, better opportunities appeared and a better me emerged.

One of my favorite songs while in college was "Stop Live in a de Pass" by Beenie Man. The song starts with the statement "when yuh live in de pass yuh lost'. The hook is

Boy, stop live down inna de past
Just remember when man a ride orse
Now yuh dead that mean yuh soul lost
Crushed like a serpent snake under grass

For those that do not understand Jamaican patois, the point of the song (to me, at least) is to move forward and win because remaining focused on the past will strip you of enjoying the beauty the future holds. Another song that I love that relates to this is Fantasia's "Lose to Win". I've experienced years of loss due to my self-esteem. I'm finally in my winning season, and guess what? You are too.

THERAPY ISN'T
A BAD THING

"You are not broken. You are breaking through."

Alex Myles

Low self-esteem is caused by a variety of issues and can reduce the quality of one's life. It can lead to serious depression and/or participating in unhealthy behavior such as alcohol and drug abuse, promiscuity, and developing an eating disorder. Or, we mistreat others. There is truth to the statement hurt people hurt people.

I never thought at the age of 14 I would need to seek therapy. I never expected to return as an adult. I sought therapy for a number of issues; one of those issues involved the need to be validated by others. I wanted to cover this in therapy because I was heading to a path of self-destruction. Could I have gotten to this point without therapy? Perhaps, but working at it alone may not work for everyone.

Talking to a professional sheds insight on how your emotions affect your daily life. It's important to acknowledge one's stressors and with the therapist's assistance, develop a strategy to minimize the stressors, or eliminate them completely. For me, the biggest challenge of therapy was trusting the process. However before trusting the process, I needed to trust the therapist.

Finding a therapist shouldn't be rushed. I was specific in seeking a woman of color, someone who could possibly relate. My therapist, in conjunction with my primary care physician (who is also a woman of color) created a treatment plan as my depression became unbearable. I really wanted to love myself, and going to therapy was a step in the right direction. In hindsight, I wished I had taken additional services such as group sessions and workshops. Utilizing the support of others going through the exact same thing would have been helpful, but thought I would make a fool of myself as I cried constantly in my one-one sessions. I did not want to cry in front of strangers.

In addition, I wished I had chronicled my journey via journaling but at the time I did not want to read on paper how much I hated myself. I thought it would make the situation worse. Recently, I received a journal as a gift and started to write on a variety of things, and I liked it. I didn't realize how therapeutic journaling could be. You don't have to write every day, but you should keep your journal with you at all times because you never know when you will have the urge to write.

I learned there are camps that assist people boost their self-esteem. It's a great concept, but not for everyone. One, it can be an expensive endeavor and two, one's work and/or family obligations may not allow one the opportunity to be away for an extended amount of time. I've considered developing my own camp, one that is affordable, fun, and with continual follow up. If anyone is interested in pursuing this endeavor, let The Curvy Doc know!

Whatever method of therapy you choose, choose wisely. Don't rush, don't feel bad about your decision to start therapy. The stigma around therapy needs to stop! I could say so much more about this, but that would require me to write a separate book. Just remember that you are not alone. You are cared for and supported; more than you know.

SHOW UP & SHOW OUT!

"I know my curves are sexy and I want everyone else to know that theirs are too. There is no reason to hide and every reason to flaunt."

Ashley Graham

I have a confession…I sometimes struggle with receiving compliments. As confident as I am, it can be strange hearing it constantly. It's great that I can encourage and motivate others, but sometimes it can be overwhelming, so overwhelming you almost want to revert back to your self-hating ways. Rome wasn't built in a day; take it one compliment at a time.

I've tested my newfound confidence in a number of ways; two experiences I will never forget. The first experience was when I did a body positivity shoot on the streets of Greensboro, North Carolina; the second when I wore a two-piece swimsuit for the first time. I need to thank my model sis, coach, owner of brands House of Sheba and Queens Chumbani Plus Keah Cher'i for providing both of these experiences. In these instances, confidence was more than just stepping out of my comfort zone, but standing tall, head up high, and knowing I looked good!

The Body Positivity Shoot: Keah recruited a number of plus size models to participate in a body positivity shoot on the streets of Greensboro, North Carolina. This shoot did not involve naked bodies, but almost as we were wearing bras and shapewear on a busy Saturday morning. Eight women from all walks of life, demonstrating self-love wearing undergarments and negative words painted on our bodies, making a statement. It was liberating! To clarify, body positivity does not have to consist of wearing minimal clothing. For me it was more about being comfortable of my body regardless of what I was wearing, and wearing only undergarments in person was my true test. I thought I was going to be nervous of everyone looking at me. Some stopped and stared; others kept on walking. The support from spectators was amazing.

Body positivity shoot (photography by Michelle Hayes)

Caption: Body positivity shoot (photography by Michelle Hayes)

The Plus-Size Woman and the Two-Piece: Every Labor Day weekend since 2009, I go on vacation as part of a large travel group. From that very first trip until 2017, I was very self-conscious of how I looked in a swimsuit. The slimmer women seemed to get all of the attention; I wanted that attention too. As much as I enjoyed these trips, I hated going to the pool or the beach. A few weeks before the trip, Keah had a "Caribbean Flava" fashion show. At the fitting, I was notified I would be wearing a two-piece swimsuit. The two-piece was a colorful, cheetah print two-piece with frills on the bra. I thought Keah was out of her mind giving me this to wear! I quickly remembered that walking in a fashion show is not about me, but the outfit. When I tried on the swimsuit, I was surprised at how I looked. I looked damn good. I couldn't stop looking in the mirror. I looked at every one of my curves, and felt oh so sexy...sexy to the point I was going to take this swimsuit with me on my vacation to Panama that Labor Day weekend. My fraternity brother who is a photographer was also going on the trip, so I scheduled a photo shoot with him; wearing my two-piece as the sun began to set.

I had my hair and makeup done a little early so I could go to the pool where my travel group was hanging out. Many of them knew my struggles so I was excited to surprise them. I walked to the pool with a smile as wide as my hips. No one couldn't tell me I didn't look fly! They loved my newfound confidence just as much as I did. Hopefully by my actions that day, I encouraged a fellow traveler who may have been afraid to wear her swimsuit with pride. By the way, the photos from the shoot came out great! My frat brother did his thing!

The infamous photo shoot in Panama
(photography by James Washington)

Caption: Photography by James Washington

Because of these two experiences, the number of times I've been told I was sexy increased. Sexy is such a strong word; definitely not on the same level as "cute" or "beautiful". I realized that sexy is a state of mind that transcends looks. Being sexy also consists of grace, poise, and most of all, confidence. Now go out there and show the world how sexy you are!

SPEAK UP!

"Never be a spectator of unfairness or stupidity. The grave will provide plenty of time for silence."

Christopher Hitchens

I love memes. They make me laugh. I stop laughing when the jokes are on people my size. See the examples below (insert fat-shaming memes here). I confess…I used to laugh at these memes too; they're posted all of the time. I began to feel guilty as I was encouraging the same things I was trying to combat. A couple of examples are below:

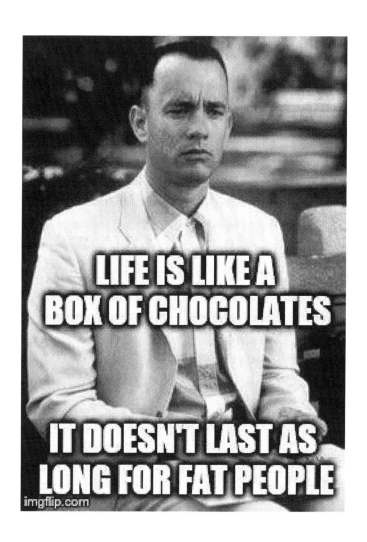

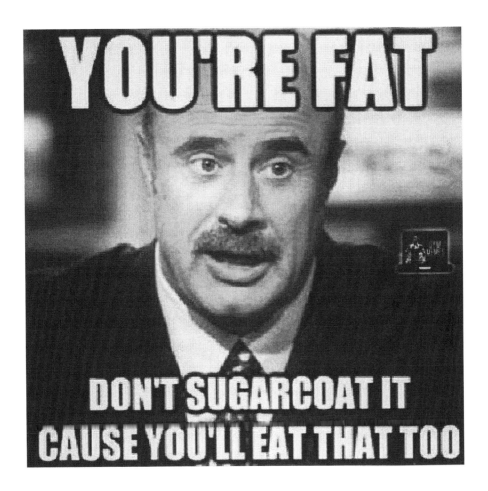

I grew up during the days of "your mama" jokes. There are many that referred to weight; no one ever thought about its impact, me included because I was young. Those jokes were more said as part of a competition, not intentionally insulting one's mother. Jokes have moved to a whole other level, a level in which they are no longer funny and can be downright damaging to one's self-esteem. I'm not saying to be the social media police; but one cannot say silent. When the jokes are focused on race, religion, and sexual orientation, folks are immediately called on it. Why have we allowed jokes regarding weight to be appropriate? They cause just as much harm as the others. Everyone isn't able to just "brush it off".

Now, when I see an inappropriate joke regarding size, I speak up. Speaking up does not have to be the length of a dissertation or even a tirade. You know your family and friends best, so choose the method that works for that relationship. Something as simple as "not cool" or "not funny" is enough. You do not want to embarrass but rather let the person be aware that what they said is hurtful. And many times hurt people, hurt people. Are their masking their insecurities, or are they trying to be cool?

My blog was the result of speaking up. A well-known entertainer was accused by many individuals of giving them sexually transmitted diseases. One of the women who came forward was plus sized. Immediately the public went in, denying she even had relations with him due to her size, and that she was not "his type". I posted about this on my Facebook page and the comments enraged me. A few men said I was prettier so people would believe me. For those who may think I'm ugly apparently wouldn't have believed me. That's sad.

It seems that there are some that presume we are unworthy of love, and anyone who sleeps with us is doing so out of pity. What the masses fail to realize is that being plus sized has become the hottest thing since sliced bread, but not always displayed in public. I've lost count of the number of times I've had men fat shame in public, but are in my inbox asking "What that mouth do?" If you can't display me in public, you sure as hell won't get the opportunity to experience all of this goodness in private.

Lastly, the terms we use to describe larger individuals...it's a matter of preference. Many bloggers and influencers say we should embrace the word "fat", basically turning a negative word into a positive. I haven't gotten there yet, but it doesn't mean I never will. I do know that I will never refer to myself as a BBW (big beautiful woman). That acronym is a porn genre and yes I'm grown but no...just...no.

Never let anyone make you feel less that. Speaking up, although tough, lifts the burden of staying silent and letting the disrespect eat you alive. If you allow the fat shaming, and laugh along to not feel like an outsider, then you're a part of the problem. A LARGE PART.

ENCOURAGE &
EMPOWER OTHERS

"The best gift you are ever going to give someone is the permission to feel safe in their own skin. To feel worthy. To feel like they are enough."

Hannah Brencher.

You've reached the pinnacle of positive self-esteem when you have shared your journey with others. The process begins with you, but should not end with you. If reading this book was your means to an end, reread the book (and I say this with love). Had I not been transparent, there would be no book. Share the wealth!

I was worried about being judged and made fun of, but little did I know so many people were watching, and I had yet to say a word. They watched me evolve, and left me messages or told me in person how proud they are of me and how much I've inspired them. Who, me? I was surprised to hear this; I'm just trying to get my life like everyone else. It's not about being humble; I'm a work in progress. I'm not where I ultimately want to be, however I'm hopeful. Being transparent was not easy, but after hearing such positive words, I had to share my story.

We tend to look up to celebrities and neglect to pay attention to the local influencers in the community making a difference. Yes, celebrities started from the bottom, but there are individuals in your circle who can learn from you (and vice versa) and will appreciate your words of wisdom. Give yourself credit!

What if you think no one is looking at you (which I highly doubt) and you're adamant about not sharing your story but still want to help others? One thing I do on social media is post inspirational quotes and articles on positive self-esteem and body image. If you're daring, facilitate a discussion on the material being shared or have a program and invite someone who shares a similar story, or a therapist to talk about the psychological impacts of self-esteem, or have a fashion show...be creative! If you're not the host, participate in body positive/positive self-esteem events. Most importantly, praise your friends making strides on their journey. Support them when they need help. Remember: You're an amazing person; let the masses know!

CONCLUSION

Congratulations you've finished the book! I hope you are feeling more confident or at least will work on taking the necessary steps to get there. Thank you for allowing me the opportunity to share my journey; know that I am here to help beyond this book!

Never forget that you are worth it! Trust the process, as it makes you who you are. Speak life into yourself; YOU ARE ENOUGH! Get rid of the negativity, whether it be words or people. Life is too short to spend another day being unkind to yourself. Your body has been there for you since day one. Love it, because it loves you.

I Would Love to Connect with You!

To bring The Curvy Doc to your city for your next event to speak visit my website at www.janellesimmons.com.

A LOVE LETTER TO J

Dear J,

Happy Valentine's Day! I wanted to let you know that you're amazing! You're not the woman I knew a few years ago. You're taking risks that many can only dream of. You're vibrant, determined, and letting the world see what you got! Don't be afraid to toot your own horn, because honey, you're doing the thing. I love the new you!

You are worthy and deserving of all of God's blessings. You are beautiful inside and out. You give love to everyone around you. There are some that won't reciprocate, and that's ok. There is someone special, watching and preparing himself for you at this very moment. He knows he cannot half-step when it comes to you. He needs to come correct or not come at all. I know a relationship is not at the top of your list, but trust me…he's watching. I see you rolling your eyes…LOL.

I don't think you realize how IMPACTFUL AND POWERFUL you are. When you speak, people listen. When you enter a room, people stop and stare. You keep saying you're just trying to get your life like everyone else, but honey, you got your life! You may not have everything you want, but you definitely have everything you need. And there are other things in store; hope you're ready to receive them.

Your dad is smiling and telling everyone in heaven how proud he is of you. I know he's been in your dreams guiding you every step of the way. That necklace of his you wear every day brings you even closer, as he feels the passion through your heartbeat. Your family and friends are cheering you on; some silently envious because that haven't gotten to the level you achieved. Don't worry about letting anyone down. You're always thinking about others, J but you have to focus...this is your season! You have a bus filled with dreams and aspirations. Those who are truly with you will board the bus; those who aren't will smell the burnt rubber of the tires as you head to your destination.

My final words to you are this, and they are very simple: I LOVE YOU, and I will continue to love you until my last breath.

From your friend for life,
The Curvy Doc

Notes_____

Notes_____

_____

_____

_____

_____

_____

_____

_____

_____

_____

_____

_____

_____

_____

_____

_____

_____

_____

_____

_____

_____

_____

_____

_____

_____

_____

Notes_____

_____

_____

_____

_____

_____

_____

_____

_____

_____

_____

_____

_____

_____

_____

_____

_____

_____

_____

_____

_____

_____

_____

_____

_____

_____

_____

_____

_____
_____
_____
_____
_____
_____
_____
_____
_____
_____
_____
_____
_____
_____
_____
_____
_____
_____
_____
_____
_____
_____
_____
_____
_____
_____
_____
_____

Notes_____

_____

_____

_____

_____

_____

_____

_____

_____

_____

_____

_____

_____

_____

_____

_____

_____

_____

_____

_____

_____

_____

_____

_____

_____

_____

_____

Made in the USA
Columbia, SC
08 July 2019